FUN SCIENCE

Experiments in
EARTH SCIENCE AND WEATHER

with Toys and Everyday Stuff

BY EMILY SOHN

Consultant:

Paul Ohmann, PhD
Associate Professor of Physics
University of St. Thomas
St. Paul, Minnesota

CAPSTONE PRESS
a capstone imprint

First Facts are published by Capstone Press,
1710 Roe Crest Drive, North Mankato, Minnesota 56003
www.capstonepub.com

Library of Congress Cataloging-in-Publication Data
Sohn, Emily.
  Experiments in earth science and weather with toys and everyday stuff / by Emily Sohn.
      pages cm—(First facts, fun science)
  Includes bibliographical references and index.
  Summary: "Step-by-step instructions for experiments pertaining to Earth Science and weather"—Provided by publisher.
  Audience: 5–8.
  Audience: K to 3.
  ISBN 978-1-4914-5035-2 (library binding)
  ISBN 978-1-4914-5075-8 (paperback)
  ISBN 978-1-4914-5079-6 (eBook PDF)
1. Earth sciences—Experiments—Juvenile literature. 2. Weather—Experiments—Juvenile literature. I. Title.
  QE29. S66 2016
  550.78—dc23   2014049479

Editorial Credits
Alesha Sullivan, editor; Kyle Grenz, designer; Jo Miller, media researcher;
Kathy McColley, production specialist

Photo Credits
Capstone Studio/Karon Dubke except: Nova Development Corporation, 19 (globes); Shutterstock: Merkushev Vasiliy, 8 (water cycle), MichaelJayBerlin, cover (push pins), Nitr, cover (towels), Petr Malyshev, cover (flashlight)

Printed in the United States of America in North Mankato, Minnesota.
052015   008823CGF15

TABLE OF CONTENTS

TURN YOUR HOME INTO A SCIENCE LAB!

Weather on Earth affects your daily life. Sun, wind, rain, or snow can change what you do and what you wear. Will you be cold? Will you get wet? Can you play at the park?

Some types of weather can also be dangerous, such as tornadoes or thunderstorms. Take a look around your house and gather up materials. Then use them to learn all about weather and science with some awesome experiments!

Safety First!

You may need an adult's help for some of these experiments. But most of them can be done on your own. If you have a question about how to do a step safely, be sure to ask an adult. Think safety first!

FLIP TO PAGE 20 TO SEE HOW THE SCIENCE WORKS IN EACH EXPERIMENT!

LET IT RAIN

Tiny water droplets in warm air cause rain to fall from the clouds. Rain helps plants and trees grow and fills lakes and rivers. But how does water get way up inside of clouds? All you need is a bathroom and some toys to find out!

Materials:

2 plastic toys, such as action figures

bathroom with a shower

2 rubber toys, such as a duck or ball

2 metal toys, such as cars

Steps:

1. With an adult's, help turn on the shower. Make the water as hot as it will go.

2. Close the door to the room. Close all windows. Turn off any fans.

3. Put one of each kind of toy on the ground. Put the others up high on a counter or ledge.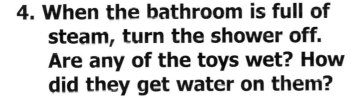

4. When the bathroom is full of steam, turn the shower off. Are any of the toys wet? How did they get water on them?

5. There should be fog on the mirror. Use your finger to draw a picture or write your name. Does your finger feel wet?

THE WATER CYCLE

Think about the huge size of our planet. Did you know water covers over 70 percent of Earth? Water fills oceans, lakes, and the ground under your feet. It falls from the sky as **precipitation**. But before it can rain or snow, water has to **evaporate**. Use washcloths to see how evaporation works!

Materials: 3 identical washcloths

Ongoing Cycle

Evaporation moves the water from lakes and puddles into the sky. Then water falls from the sky as rain or snow. This is called the water cycle.

Steps:

1. **In a sink soak all of the washcloths. Then squeeze out any extra water.**

2. **Hang one wet washcloth in the sunlight outside. Hang one in the shade outside. Hang the last one in the bathroom inside your home.**

3. **Check on the washcloths every 10 minutes. Which one dries the fastest? Which takes the longest to dry? Where did the water go?**

precipitation—water that falls from the clouds in the form of rain, hail, or snow

evaporate—to change from a liquid to a gas

THE BEAUTY OF RAINBOWS

Rainbows are pretty! They can also teach us about light and weather. As sunlight goes through a raindrop, the light is sorted into rainbow colors. You may know the colors of the rainbow—red, orange, yellow, green, blue, indigo, and violet.

You can create a rainbow in your house too! Use a glass of water to sort light into colors.

Materials:

water

clear glass

a piece of white paper

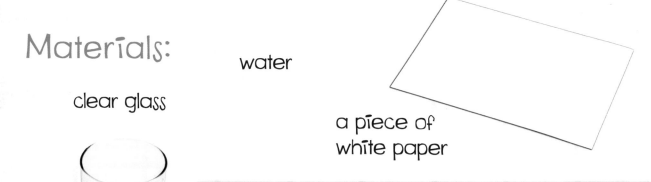

Why Is the Sky Blue?

The air is full of dust and other specks. Sunlight bounces off these specks. On a color **spectrum**, blue light spreads out the best. So on a clear day, we see a blue sky.

Steps:

1. **Place a piece of paper in front of a window on a ledge or table.**

2. **Fill a clear glass with water. The water should be about 1 inch (2.5 centimeters) from the top of the glass.** ●••••••••••••••••••••••••

3. **Hold the glass just above the paper so the sunlight shines through it. Be careful not to spill! The rays of sunlight should hit the paper. The water bends the sunlight. What do you see on the paper? Do you see rainbow colors?** ●•••••••••••••••••••

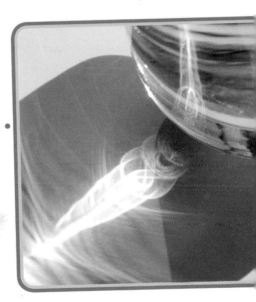

Tip:

You may need to move the glass or paper to get the light to hit just right.

spectrum—the range of colors that is shown when light shines through drops of water

11

BLOWN AWAY!

Wind can help you fly a kite. Wind can also move a sailboat across the water. Wind comes from sunlight heating the **atmosphere**, causing air to flow. Make a pinwheel to learn more about the power of wind!

Materials:

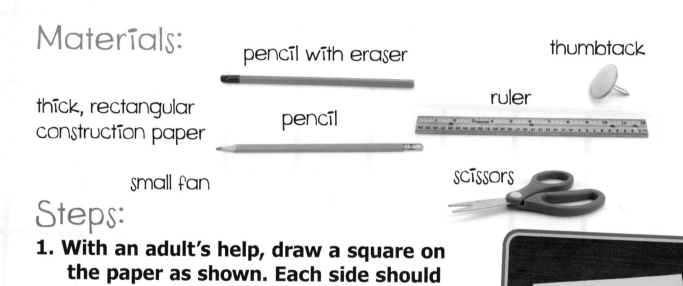

pencil with eraser

thumbtack

thick, rectangular construction paper

pencil

ruler

small fan

scissors

Steps:

1. **With an adult's help, draw a square on the paper as shown. Each side should be 4 inches (10 cm) long. Then cut the square out of the construction paper.**

atmosphere—the mixture of gases that surrounds Earth

12

2. **Cut toward the center of the square from each corner. Be sure not to cut all the way to the center. Ask an adult to use a thumbtack to poke holes in every other corner and middle of the square.**

3. **Curl the corners with holes toward the center. Have an adult push the pin through all five holes. Attach the pin to the pencil's eraser. Make it loose enough so the pinwheel can turn.**

4. **Hold your pinwheel outside or so it faces a fan. Does it spin? What happens if you turn the pinwheel sideways? How can you hold it to make the wheel spin fastest?**

Fact:

Wind turbines work similar to a pinwheel. Wind moves large blades that generate electricity to power nearby towns and cities.

TWISTER!

Beneath a dark thunderstorm, a thick **funnel cloud** forms. The wind inside of that cloud whips at speeds up to 300 miles (483 kilometers) per hour. It howls and spins. This is how a tornado begins! Tornadoes can destroy houses and topple trees. Use two empty bottles to make your own twister!

Materials:

strong tape, such as duct tape

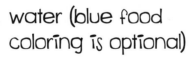

water (blue food coloring is optional)

2 empty 2-liter soda bottles

funnel cloud—a cone-shaped cloud that is usually a visible part of a tornado

Steps:

1. Remove the caps from both bottles.

2. Pour water into one of the bottles. Fill the bottle more than half full but not all the way full. Leave the other bottle empty. ●

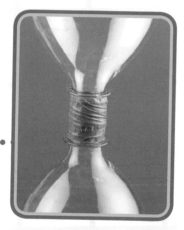

3. Turn the empty bottle upside down. Line it up with the other bottle so the openings meet. Tape the necks together tightly. ●

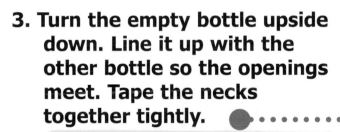

Tip:
Have an adult help you hold the two bottles together while you tape.

4. Turn the bottles over. The bottle with water in it should be on the top. Quickly, give the bottles a little swirl. Look inside. Do you see a funnel that looks like a tornado? ●

ELECTRIC SKY

There is **electricity** in the sky, especially during a storm. Electricity flows between clouds. Or it can flow between a cloud and the ground. This is known as **lightning**.

Lightning looks like a flash, and it sometimes fills the sky with bright light. Try to make some mini lightning of your own!

Materials:

scissors

aluminum pie tin

flat piece of Styrofoam, at least as big as your hand

tape

Flying Sparks!

There are other ways to make mini lightning bolts! Put socks on, and shuffle your feet on a rug. Touch a metal object with one finger. Kazam! Be ready to feel a mini electric shock!

electricity—movement of electrons that can be used to make light and heat or to make machines work
lightning—the electricity caused by friction in a cloud

Steps:

1. With an adult's help, use scissors to cut a thin strip from the Styrofoam.

2. Tape the strip of Styrofoam to the inside of the pie tin. This will be the handle.

3. Rub the large piece of the Styrofoam all over your hair. Rub really fast!

4. Set the large piece of Styrofoam down on a table. The part that touched your hair should face up.

5. Use the handle to pick up the pie tin. Hold it about 1 foot (0.3 meter) above the Styrofoam, and let it drop.

6. Carefully touch the pie tin with the tip of your finger. Did you feel a spark?

SEASONAL DIFFERENCES

Is the weather hot or cold where you live? It could be both! We often plan our lives around seasons. During winter months kids can go sledding. In the summer it's common to swim in pools to cool off.

Earth spins, which tells us if it's day or night. While the Earth spins, it **orbits** the Sun too. This orbiting tells us what time of the year it is. Use toys to learn more about seasons!

Materials:

washable marker

big yellow ball

small blue ball

Steps:

1. **Place the yellow ball on a table. This is the Sun.**

orbit—to travel around an object in space

18

2. Draw a small dot on the blue ball. The blue ball is Earth, and the dot is the North Pole. ●·············

3. Hold Earth so the North Pole is tilted toward the Sun. If you live on the northern half of the globe, this means it's summer. Your home faces the Sun. ●········

4. Walk around the table so you're on the other side of the Sun. You are in orbit. Keep the Earth leaning the same way. Now it is winter. Your home faces away from the Sun, and it's colder outside. ●·············

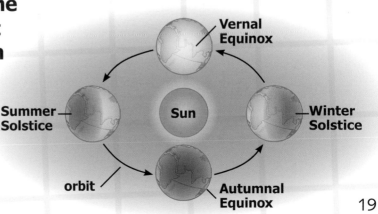

5. Pretend you live near the South Pole. How might the seasons differ from where you live now?

Vernal Equinox

Summer Solstice

Sun

Winter Solstice

orbit

Autumnal Equinox

WHY IT WORKS

Are you wondering how these amazing experiments worked? Here is the science behind the fun!

PAGE 6 - LET IT RAIN

Steam is **water vapor** in the air. When the warm water touched the cool toys, it changed from gas form to a liquid.

PAGE 8 - THE WATER CYCLE

The washcloth in the sunlight should have dried the quickest because of the Sun's heat. The Sun's heat made the water turn into a gas, which is known as evaporation.

PAGE 10 - THE BEAUTY OF RAINBOWS

Rainbows form when sunlight bends as it passes through drops of water. The light acted the same when it passed through your glass of water. The light was sorted into pretty rainbow colors.

PAGE 12 - BLOWN AWAY!

When the wind blows on the blades of your pinwheel, they spin. Wind is sometimes used to create clean power instead of using gas or oil to make electricity.

PAGE 14 - TWISTER!

In the experiment swirling the bottles forms a **vortex**, similar to spinning air in a system of thunderstorms.

PAGE 16 - ELECTRIC SKY

When you rubbed the Styrofoam on your hair, you pulled **electrons** onto the piece of Styrofoam. These electrons then moved onto the pie tin when they touched. When your finger touched the metal pie tin, some electrons created a mini spark of electricity.

PAGE 18 - SEASONAL DIFFERENCES

It takes six months for Earth to move from one side of the Sun to the opposite side. And it takes one full year to go all the way around the Sun. When it is summer in the northern half of the globe, it is winter in the southern half.

water vapor—water in gas form
vortex—air moving in a circular motion
electron—one of the tiny particles that make up all
    things; protons and neutrons also make up all things

GLOSSARY

atmosphere (AT-muh-sfeer)—the mixture of gases that surrounds Earth

electricity (i-lek-TRISS-uh-tee)—movement of electrons that can be used to make light and heat or to make machines work

electron (i-LEK-tron)—one of the tiny particles that make up all things; protons and neutrons also make up all things

evaporate (i-VA-puh-rayt)—to change from a liquid to a gas

funnel cloud (FUHN-uhl KLOUD)—a cone-shaped cloud that is usually a visible part of a tornado

lightning (LITE-ning)—the electricity caused by friction in a cloud

orbit (OR-bit)—to travel around an object in space

precipitation (pri-sip-i-TAY-shuhn)—water that falls from the clouds in the form of rain, hail, or snow

spectrum (SPEK-truhm)—the range of colors that is shown when light shines through drops of water

vortex (VOHR-tex)—air moving in a circular motion

water vapor (WAH-tur VAY-pur)—water in gas form

READ MORE

Furgang, Kathy. *Everything Weather.* National Geographic Kids. Washington, D.C.: National Geographic, 2012.

Ganeri, Anita. *Wild Weather.* Extreme Nature. Chicago: Raintree, 2013.

Rustad, Martha E.H. *Tornadoes: Be Aware and Prepare.* Weather Aware. North Mankato, Minn.: Capstone Press, 2015.

INTERNET SITES

FactHound offers a safe, fun way to find Internet sites related to this book. All of the sites on FactHound have been researched by our staff.

Here's all you do:

Visit *www.facthound.com*

Type in this code: 9781491450352

Check out projects, games and lots more at
www.capstonekids.com

INDEX